little for BIG OCCASIONS

Only have minutes to sew? Get started on any one of these fun little quilts for special occasions, and you'll complete it in just a few quick sessions of appliqué, machine embroidery, and quilting. From birthday cupcakes to July 4th firecrackers or Christmas packages, you can put together seven sweet themes to display on tables or walls. When time is of the essence, Sandi Colwell's lighthearted designs finish fast!

meet sandi Colwell

Sandi Colwell crafts, blogs, and records podcasts for the visitors to her Web site, yet the Massachusetts resident still finds time to whip up new quilt designs.

"I come from a long line of women who enjoy quilting and sewing," says Sandi, "but I was uninterested until I became a mother. My grandmother had given each of her granddaughters a sewing machine for high school graduation. I left mine unopened in the closet. My mother's machine had broken, and she asked to use mine. So I blew the dust off the machine and gave it to my mother. And then I thought, "Maybe it would be fun to learn to sew." The first thing I made was a child's apron for my daughter. Several years after that, I got the quilting bug from a TV quilting show. Now my mom and I attend the same quilt guild and enjoy shopping for fabric together."

Sandi has seen her quilts and quilting articles published in several national magazines. To visit Sandi online, go to quiltcabanapatterns.com, where you can get the latest news about her quilting career and see more of her colorful designs.

LEISURE ARTS, INC.
Little Rock, Arkansas

valentine love

Finished Wall Hanging Size:
21¹/₂" x 17¹/₂" (55 cm x 44 cm)

fabric requirements

Yardage is based on 43"/44" (109 cm/112 cm) wide fabric. A fat quarter measures approximately 18" x 22" (46 cm x 56 cm).

- $1/2$ yd (46 cm) of red print fabric for borders and binding
- Fat quarter of purple print fabric for backgrounds and hearts
- Fat quarter of light pink print fabric for backgrounds
- Scrap of dark pink print fabric for hearts
- Scrap of black solid fabric for letters
- 23" x 19" (58 cm x 48 cm) piece of muslin for backing

You will also need:
- 23" x 19" (58 cm x 48 cm) piece of batting
- Paper-backed fusible web

cutting the pieces

*Follow **Rotary Cutting**, page 22, to cut fabric. Cut borders and binding strips across the selvage-to-selvage width of the fabric. All measurements include $1/4$" seam allowances.*

From red print fabric:
- Cut 2 **side borders** 2" x 14".
- Cut 2 **top/bottom borders** 2" x 21".
- Cut 3 **binding strips** $2^1/2$" wide.

From purple print fabric:
- Cut 2 **rectangles** $9^1/4$" x $7^1/4$".

From light pink print fabric:
- Cut 2 **rectangles** $9^1/4$" x $7^1/4$".

cutting the appliqués

*Follow **Preparing Fusible Appliqués**, page 23, to make appliqués from patterns, page 16.*

From purple print fabric:
- Cut 2 **hearts**.

From dark pink print fabric:
- Cut 2 **hearts**.

From black solid fabric:
- Cut **letters** LOVE.

assembling the background

*Follow **Machine Piecing** and **Pressing**, page 23. Match right sides and use a $1/4$" seam allowance.*

1. Sew 1 purple **rectangle** and 1 light pink **rectangle** together to make **Unit 1**. Press seam allowances toward the darker fabric. Make 2 Unit 1's.

Unit 1 (make 2)

2. Sew **Unit 1's** together to make background.

assembling the quilt

*Refer to **Assembling the Quilt**, page 23, to assemble, layer, and appliqué the wall hanging. Quilt in the ditch between the borders and quilt top center.*

completing the quilt

1. Follow **Adding a Hanging Sleeve**, page 25, to make and attach a hanging sleeve.
2. Follow **Attaching Binding with Mitered Corners**, page 25, to bind wall hanging using **binding strips**. •

celebrate

Finished Wall Hanging Size:
21" x 17½" (53 cm x 44 cm)

fabric requirements

Yardage is based on 43"/44" (109 cm/112 cm) wide fabric. A fat quarter measures approximately 18" x 22" (46 cm x 56 cm).

$5/8$ yd (57 cm) of pink print fabric for sashing, borders, binding and cupcake tops

Fat quarter of yellow print fabric for background

Fat quarter of aqua print fabric for background

Scrap of brown print fabric for letters

Scrap of red solid fabric for cherries

Scrap of brown print fabric for cupcake cups

$22^1/2$" x 19" (57 cm x 48 cm) piece of muslin for backing

You will also need:

$22^1/2$" x 19" (57 cm x 48 cm) piece of batting

Paper-backed fusible web

cutting the pieces

*Follow **Rotary Cutting**, page 22, to cut fabric. Cut sashing, borders, and binding strips across the selvage-to-selvage width of the fabric. All measurements include $1/4$" seam allowances.*

From pink print fabric:

- Cut 1 **sashing** 3" x $17^1/2$".
- Cut 2 **side borders** 2" x 14".
- Cut 2 **top/bottom borders** 2" x $20^1/2$".
- Cut 3 **binding strips** $2^1/2$" wide.

From yellow print fabric:

- Cut 2 **rectangles** $6^1/4$" x 6".
- Cut 1 **square** 6" x 6".

From aqua print fabric:

- Cut 2 **rectangles** $6^1/4$" x 6".
- Cut 1 **square** 6" x 6".

cutting the appliqués

*Follow **Preparing Fusible Appliqués**, page 23, to make appliqués from patterns, page 17.*

From pink print fabric:

- Cut 6 **cupcake tops**.

From brown print fabric:

- Cut **letters** CELEBRATE.

From red print fabric:

- Cut 6 **cherries**.

From brown print fabric:

- Cut 6 **cupcake cups**.

assembling the background

*Follow **Machine Piecing** and **Pressing**, page 23. Match right sides and use a $1/4$" seam allowance.*

1. Sew 2 yellow **rectangles** and 1 aqua **square** together to make **Unit 1**. Sew 2 aqua **rectangles** and 1 yellow **square** together to make **Unit 2**. Press seam allowances toward the darker fabric.

Unit 1

Unit 2

2. Sew **Unit 1**, **Unit 2**, and **sashing** together to make background. Press seam allowances away from sashing.

assembling the quilt

*Refer to **Assembling the Quilt**, page 23, to assemble, layer, and appliqué the wall hanging. Letters and cherries are not blanket stitched. Quilt in the ditch along each side of the sashing.*

completing the quilt

1. Follow **Adding a Hanging Sleeve**, page 25, to make and attach a hanging sleeve.
2. Follow **Attaching Binding with Mitered Corners**, page 25, to bind wall hanging using **binding strips**. •

easter delight

Finished Wall Hanging Size:
21" x 17$\frac{1}{2}$" (53 cm x 44 cm)

fabric requirements

Yardage is based on 43"/44" (109 cm/112 cm) wide fabric. A fat quarter measures approximately 18" x 22" (46 cm x 56 cm).

> ¹/₂ yd (46 cm) of purple print fabric for borders, binding, egg, and tulip
>
> Fat quarter of light green print for backgrounds
>
> Fat quarter of light blue print fabric for background
>
> Scrap of medium green print fabric for stems, leaves, and egg stripe
>
> Scrap of yellow print fabric for egg, egg stripes, and tulips
>
> Scraps of assorted pink print fabrics for tulips, egg, egg stripes, and bunnies
>
> 22¹/₂" x 19" (57 cm x 48 cm) piece of muslin for backing

You will also need:

> 22¹/₂" x 19" (57 cm x 48 cm) piece of batting
>
> Paper-backed fusible web
>
> Purple embroidery floss

cutting the pieces

*Follow **Rotary Cutting**, page 22, to cut fabric. Cut borders and binding strips across the selvage-to-selvage width of the fabric. All measurements include ¹/₄" seam allowances.*

From purple print fabric:

> Cut 2 **side borders** 2" x 14".
>
> Cut 2 **top/bottom borders** 2" x 20¹/₂".
>
> Cut 3 **binding strips** 2¹/₂" wide.

From light green print fabric:

> Cut 2 **rectangles** 4¹/₂" x 17¹/₂".

From light blue print fabric:

> Cut 1 **rectangle** 6" x 17¹/₂".

cutting the appliqués

*Follow **Preparing Fusible Appliqués**, page 23, to make appliqués from patterns, pages 17 and 18.*

From purple print fabric:

> Cut 1 **egg**.
>
> Cut 1 **tulip**.

From medium green print fabric:

> Cut 1 **large egg stripe**.
>
> Cut 5 **stems**.
>
> Cut 5 **leaf sets**.

From yellow print fabric:

> Cut 1 **egg**.
>
> Cut 1 **egg stripe set**.
>
> Cut 2 **tulips**.

From assorted pink print fabric:

> Cut 3 **bunnies**.
>
> Cut 2 **tulips**.
>
> Cut 1 **egg**.
>
> Cut 1 **egg stripe set**.

assembling the background

*Follow **Machine Piecing** and **Pressing**, page 23. Match right sides and use a ¹/₄" seam allowance.*

1. Sew **rectangles** together to make background. Press seam allowances toward darker fabric.

assembling the quilt

*Refer to **Assembling the Quilt**, page 23, to assemble, layer, and appliqué the wall hanging.*

completing the quilt

1. Use 6 strands of embroidery floss to make French Knots for the bunnies' eyes.
2. Follow **Adding a Hanging Sleeve**, page 25, to make and attach a hanging sleeve.
3. Follow **Attaching Binding with Mitered Corners**, page 25, to bind wall hanging using **binding strips**. •

french knot

Follow **Figs. 1 – 4** to complete French Knots. Come up at 1. Wrap thread once around needle and insert needle at 2, holding end of thread with non-stitching fingers. Tighten knot, then pull needle through, holding floss until it must be released.

Fig. 1	Fig. 2

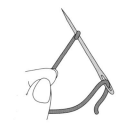

Fig. 3	Fig. 4

let freedom ring

Finished Wall Hanging Size:
21" x 17¹/₂" (53 cm x 44 cm)

fabric requirements

Yardage is based on 43"/44" (109 cm/112 cm) wide fabric. A fat quarter measures approximately 18" x 22" (46 cm x 56 cm).

- $^1/_2$ yd (46 cm) of dark blue print fabric for borders, binding, and stripe
- Fat quarter of light blue print fabric for background
- Fat quarter of dark red print fabric for firecrackers
- Scrap of light red print fabric for stripe
- Scrap of white print fabric for stripe
- Scrap of gold print fabric for stars
- 22$^1/_2$" x 19" (57 cm x 48 cm) piece of muslin for backing

You will also need:

- 22$^1/_2$" x 19" (57 cm x 48 cm) piece of batting
- Paper-backed fusible web

cutting the pieces

*Follow **Rotary Cutting**, page 22, to cut fabric. Cut borders and binding strips across the selvage-to-selvage width of the fabric. All measurements include $^1/_4$" seam allowances.*

From dark blue print fabric:
- Cut 2 **side borders** 2" x 14".
- Cut 2 **top/bottom borders** 2" x 20$^1/_2$".
- Cut 3 **binding strips** 2$^1/_2$" wide.

From light blue print fabric:
- Cut **background** 17$^1/_2$" x 14".

cutting the appliqués

*Follow **Preparing Fusible Appliqués**, page 23, to make appliqués from patterns, page 18.*

From dark blue print fabric:
- Cut 1 **stripe**.

From dark red print fabric:
- Cut 5 **firecrackers**.

From light red print fabric:
- Cut 1 **stripe**.

From white print fabric:
- Cut 1 **stripe**.

From gold print fabric:
- Cut 5 **stars**.

assembling the quilt

*Refer to **Assembling the Quilt**, page 23, to assemble, layer, and appliqué the wall hanging. Quilt in the ditch between the borders and quilt top center.*

completing the quilt

1. Follow **Adding a Hanging Sleeve**, page 25, to make and attach a hanging sleeve.
2. Follow **Attaching Binding with Mitered Corners**, page 25, to bind wall hanging using **binding strips**. •

trick or treat

Finished Wall Hanging Size:
21" x 17¹/₂" (53 cm x 44 cm)

fabric requirements

Yardage is based on 43"/44" (109 cm/112 cm) wide fabric. A fat quarter measures approximately 18" x 22" (46 cm x 56 cm).

- ⅝ yd (57 cm) of black solid fabric for borders and binding
- Fat quarter of purple print fabric for background
- Fat quarter of black print fabric for treat bags
- Scrap of green print fabric for stripe and letters
- Scraps of orange, green, and yellow print fabrics for candy
- Scraps of white, orange, and yellow print fabrics for candy corn
- 22½" x 19" (57 cm x 48 cm) piece of muslin for backing

You will also need:

- 22½" x 19" (57 cm x 48 cm) piece of batting
- Paper-backed fusible web

cutting the pieces

*Follow **Rotary Cutting**, page 22, to cut fabric. Cut borders and binding strips across the selvage-to-selvage width of the fabric. All measurements include ¼" seam allowances.*

From black solid fabric:
- Cut 2 **side borders** 2" x 14".
- Cut 2 **top/bottom borders** 2" x 20½".
- Cut 3 **binding strips** 2½" wide.

From purple print fabric:
- Cut **background** 17½" x 14".

From *each* of white, orange, and yellow print fabrics:
- Cut 1 **strip** 1½" x 12".

cutting the appliqués

*Follow **Preparing Fusible Appliqués**, page 23, to make appliqués from patterns, page 19.*

From black print fabric:
- Cut 3 **treat bags**.

From green print fabric:
- Cut **letters** TRICK OR TREAT.
- Cut **stripe** 1" x 17½".

From *each* of orange and yellow print fabrics:
- Cut 1 **candy**.

From green print fabric:
- Cut 2 **candies**.

assembling the quilt

*Refer to **Assembling the Quilt**, page 23, to assemble, layer, and appliqué the wall hanging. For candy corn appliqués, sew strips together along long edges before making appliqués. After tracing appliqué on fusible web, place the fusible web on the wrong side of the fabrics over the strips so that each color is shown on the finished appliqué. Letters are not blanket stitched. Quilt in the ditch between the borders and wall hanging top center.*

completing the quilt

1. Follow **Adding a Hanging Sleeve**, page 25, to make and attach a hanging sleeve.
2. Follow **Attaching Binding with Mitered Corners**, page 25, to bind wall hanging using **binding strips**. •

thanksgiving

Finished Wall Hanging Size:
21" x 17¹/₂" (53 cm x 44 cm)

fabric requirements

Yardage is based on 43"/44" (109 cm/112 cm) wide fabric. A fat quarter measures approximately 18" x 22" (46 cm x 56 cm).

- 1/2 yd (46 cm) of brown print fabric for borders and binding
- Fat quarter of green print fabric for backgrounds, leaves, and stems
- Fat quarter of cranberry print fabric for backgrounds, pie tin, steam holes, cherry, feathers, and wattle
- Scrap of brown print fabric for body and acorn bottoms
- Scrap of dark brown print fabric for acorn tops
- Scrap of beige print fabric for piecrust
- Scrap of orange print fabric for pumpkins and feathers
- Scrap of yellow print fabric for feather, beak, and feet
- 22 1/2" x 19" (57 cm x 48 cm) piece of muslin for backing

You will also need:

- 22 1/2" x 19" (57 cm x 48 cm) piece of batting
- Paper-backed fusible web
- Two 1/2" (13 mm) green buttons

cutting the pieces

Follow Rotary Cutting, page 22, to cut fabric. Cut borders and binding strips across the selvage-to-selvage width of the fabric. All measurements include 1/4" seam allowances.

From brown print fabric:
- Cut 2 **side borders** 2" x 14".
- Cut 2 **top/bottom borders** 2" x 20 1/2".
- Cut 3 **binding strips** 2 1/2" wide.

From green print fabric:
- Cut 2 **rectangles** 9" x 7 1/4".

From cranberry print fabric:
- Cut 2 **rectangles** 9" x 7 1/4".

cutting the appliqués

Follow Preparing Fusible Appliqués, page 23, to make appliqués from patterns, pages 19 and 20.

From green print fabric:
- Cut 2 **leaves**.
- Cut 2 **stems**.

From cranberry print fabric:
- Cut 1 **pie tin**.
- Cut 3 **steam holes**.
- Cut 1 **cherry**.
- Cut 2 **turkey feathers**.
- Cut 1 **turkey wattle**.

From brown print fabric:
- Cut 2 **acorn bottoms**.
- Cut 1 **turkey body**.

From dark brown print fabric:
- Cut 2 **acorn tops**.

From beige print fabric:
- Cut 1 **piecrust**.

From orange print fabric:
- Cut 1 **large pumpkin**.
- Cut 1 **small pumpkin**.
- Cut 2 **turkey feathers**.

From yellow print fabric:
- Cut 1 **turkey feather**.
- Cut 1 **turkey beak**.
- Cut 2 **turkey feet**.

assembling the background

Follow Machine Piecing and Pressing, page 23. Match right sides and use a 1/4" seam allowance.

1. Sew 1 cranberry **rectangle** and 1 green **rectangle** together to make **Unit 1**. Press seam allowances toward the darker fabric. Make 2 Unit 1's.

Unit 1 (make 2)

2. Sew **Unit 1's** together to make background.

assembling the quilt

Refer to Assembling the Quilt, page 23, to assemble, layer, and appliqué the wall hanging. Beak is straight stitched around edges; wattle and steam holes are zigzag stitched through the center. Quilt in the ditch between the borders and wall hanging top center.

completing the quilt

1. Follow **Adding a Hanging Sleeve**, page 25, to make and attach a hanging sleeve.
2. Follow **Attaching Binding with Mitered Corners**, page 25, to bind wall hanging using **binding strips**. •

ho ho ho

Finished Wall Hanging Size:
21" x 17¹/₂" (53 cm x 44 cm)

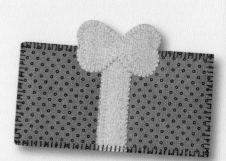

fabric requirements

Yardage is based on 43"/44" (109 cm/112 cm) wide fabric. A fat quarter measures approximately 18" x 22" (46 cm x 56 cm).

> $1/2$ yd (46 cm) of dark green print fabric for borders and binding
>
> Fat quarter of dark red print fabric for backgrounds and letters
>
> Fat quarter of gold print fabric for background, gift, bows, and bulbs
>
> Scrap of light green print fabric for gifts, bow, and bulbs
>
> $22^1/2$" x 19" (57 cm x 48 cm) piece of muslin for backing

You will also need:

> $22^1/2$" x 19" (57 cm x 48 cm) piece of batting
>
> Paper-backed fusible web
>
> Green double-fold bias tape

cutting the pieces

*Follow **Rotary Cutting**, page 22, to cut fabric. Cut borders and binding strips across the selvage-to-selvage width of the fabric. All measurements include $1/4$" seam allowances.*

From dark green print fabric:
> Cut 2 **side borders** 2" x 14".
> Cut 2 **top/bottom borders** 2" x $20^1/2$".
> Cut 3 **binding strips** $2^1/2$" wide.

From dark red print fabric:
> Cut 2 **rectangles** $4^1/2$" x $17^1/2$".

From gold print fabric:
> Cut 1 **rectangle** 6" x $17^1/2$".

cutting the appliqués

*Follow **Preparing Fusible Appliqués**, page 23, to make appliqués from patterns, page 21.*

From dark red print fabric:
> Cut 3 **letters** H.
> Cut 3 **letters** O.

From gold print fabric:
> Cut 2 **bulbs**.
> Cut 1 **tall gift**.
> Cut 2 **short ribbons**.
> Cut 2 **bows**.

From light green print fabric:
> Cut 2 **bulbs**.
> Cut 2 **short gifts**.
> Cut 1 **long ribbon**.
> Cut 1 **bow**.

assembling the background

*Follow **Machine Piecing** and **Pressing**, page 23. Match right sides and use a $1/4$" seam allowance.*

1. Sew 2 dark red **rectangles** and 1 gold **rectangle** together to make **background**. Press seam allowances toward the darker fabric.
2. Sew bias tape to background approximately 1" from top for light cord.

assembling the quilt

*Refer to **Assembling the Quilt**, page 23, to assemble, layer, and appliqué the wall hanging. Quilt in the ditch between the borders and wall hanging top center.*

completing the quilt

1. Follow **Adding a Hanging Sleeve**, page 25, to make and attach a hanging sleeve.
2. Follow **Attaching Binding with Mitered Corners**, page 25, to bind wall hanging using **binding strips**. •

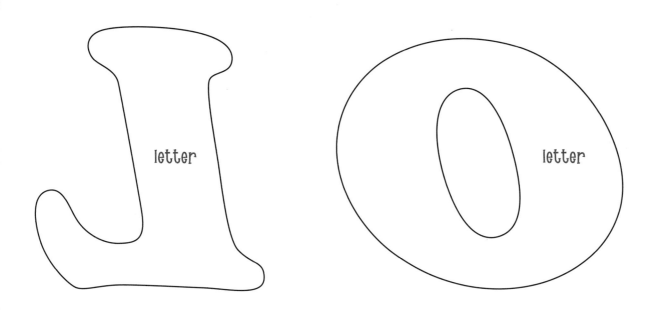

letter

letter

valentine love
page 2

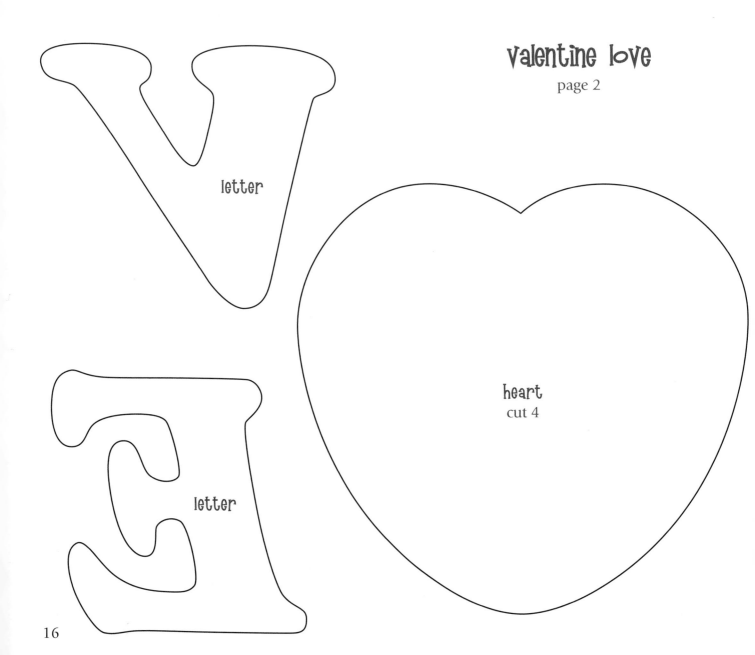

letter

heart
cut 4

letter

cupcake top
cut 6

cupcake cup
cut 6

letters
cut 3 of "E";
cut 1 of each
remaining letter

cherry
cut 6

celebrate
page 4

bunny
cut 3

easter delight
page 6

egg
cut 3

egg stripe set
cut 2

large egg stripe
cut 1

17

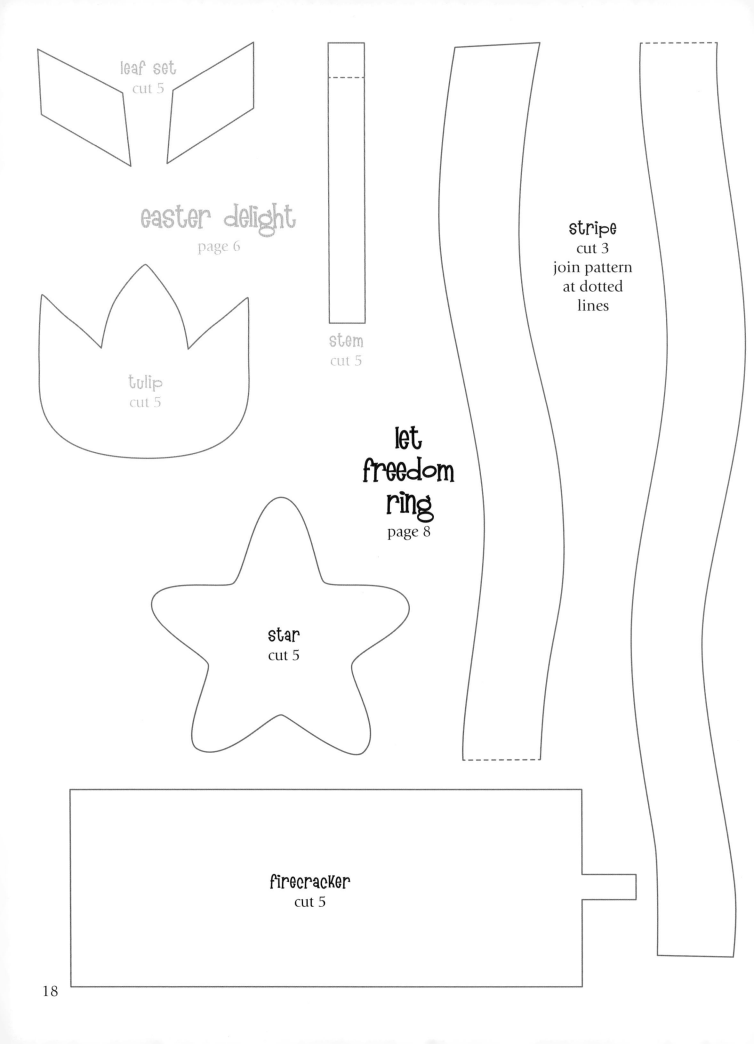

leaf set
cut 5

easter delight
page 6

stem
cut 5

stripe
cut 3
join pattern
at dotted
lines

tulip
cut 5

let
freedom
ring
page 8

star
cut 5

firecracker
cut 5

trick or treat
page 10

candy corn
cut 5

turkey feather
cut 5

treat bag
cut 3

thanksgiving
page 12

turkey foot
cut 2

turkey beak
cut 1

turkey wattle
cut 1

cherry
cut 1

letters
cut 3 each of
"T" and "R";
cut 1 each of
remaining letters

stem
cut 2

steam hole
cut 3

candy
cut 4

leaf
cut 2

acorn top
cut 2

turkey body
cut 1

piecrust
cut 1

acorn bottom
cut 2

pie tin
cut 1

thanksgiving
page 12

large pumpkin
cut 1

small pumpkin
cut 1

20

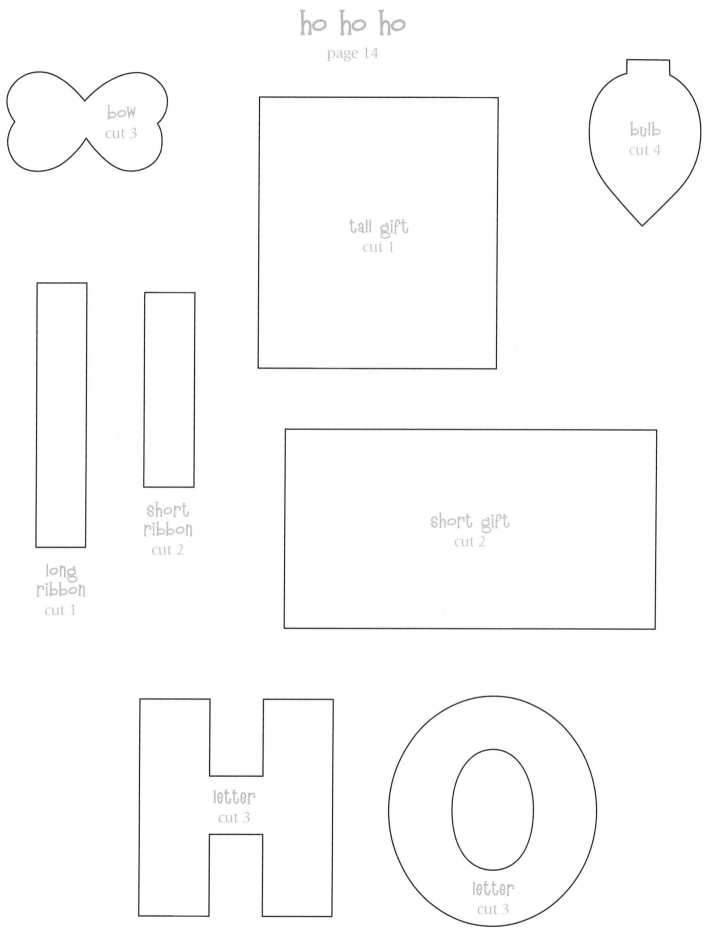

bow
cut 3

tall gift
cut 1

bulb
cut 4

short
ribbon
cut 2

long
ribbon
cut 1

short gift
cut 2

letter
cut 3

letter
cut 3

To make your quilting easier and more enjoyable, we encourage you to carefully read all of the general instructions, study the color photographs, and familiarize yourself with the individual project instructions before beginning a project.

fabrics

SELECTING FABRICS

Choose high-quality, medium-weight 100% cotton fabrics. All-cotton fabrics hold a crease better, fray less, and are easier to quilt than cotton/polyester blends.

Yardage requirements listed for each project are based on 43"/44" wide fabric with a "usable" width of 40" after shrinkage and trimming selvages. Actual usable width will probably vary slightly from fabric to fabric. Our recommended yardage lengths should be adequate for occasional re-squaring of fabric when many cuts are required.

PREPARING FABRICS

We recommend that all fabrics be washed, dried, and pressed before cutting. If fabrics are not pre-washed, washing the finished quilt will cause shrinkage and give it a more "antique" look and feel. Bright and dark colors, which may run, should always be washed before cutting. After washing and drying fabric, fold lengthwise with wrong sides together and matching selvages.

rotary cutting

CUTTING FROM FAT QUARTERS

- Unfold fat quarter and place on work surface with short edge closest to you.

- Cut all strips parallel to the longer edge of the fabric.

- To cut each strip required for a project, place ruler over left edge of fabric, aligning desired marking on ruler with left edge; make cut.

CUTTING FROM YARDAGE

- Place fabric on work surface with fold closest to you.

- Cut all strips from the selvage-to-selvage width of the fabric unless otherwise indicated in project instructions.

- Square left edge of fabric using rotary cutter and rulers (**Figs. 1 – 2**).

Fig. 1   **Fig. 2**

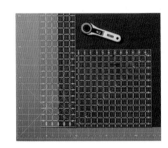 

- To cut each strip required for a project, place ruler over cut edge of fabric, aligning desired marking on ruler with cut edge; make cut (**Fig. 3**).

Fig. 3

- When cutting several strips from a single piece of fabric, it is important to make sure that cuts remain at a perfect right angle to the fold; square fabric as needed.

preparing fusible appliqués

White or light-colored fabrics may need to be lined with fusible interfacing before applying fusible web to prevent darker fabrics from showing through.

1. Place paper-backed fusible web, paper side up, over appliqué pattern. Trace pattern onto paper side of web with pencil as many times as indicated in project instructions for a single fabric.
2. Follow manufacturer's instructions to fuse traced patterns to wrong side of fabrics. Do not remove paper backing. (*Note:* Some pieces may be given as measurements, such as a 2" x 4" rectangle, instead of drawn patterns. Fuse web to wrong side of fabrics indicated for these pieces.)
3. Use scissors to cut out appliqué pieces along traced lines; use rotary cutting equipment to cut out appliqué pieces given as measurements. Remove paper backing from all pieces.

machine piecing

Precise cutting, followed by accurate piecing, will ensure that all pieces of quilt top fit together well.

- Set sewing machine stitch length for approximately 11 stitches per inch.

- Use neutral-colored general-purpose sewing thread (not quilting thread) in needle and in bobbin.

- An accurate $^1/_4$" seam allowance is *essential*. Presser feet that are $^1/_4$" wide are available for most sewing machines.

- When piecing, always place pieces right sides together and match raw edges; pin if necessary.

- When sewing across intersection of two seams, match seams exactly, making sure seam allowances are pressed in opposite directions (**Fig. 4**).

Fig. 4

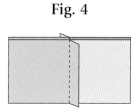

pressing

- Use steam iron set on "Cotton" for all pressing.

- Press after sewing each seam.

- Seam allowances are almost always pressed to one side, usually toward darker fabric. However, to reduce bulk it may occasionally be necessary to press seam allowances toward the lighter fabric or even to press them open.

- To prevent dark fabric seam allowance from showing through light fabric, trim darker seam allowance slightly narrower than lighter seam allowance.

assembling the quilt

*Refer to **Machine Piecing** and **Pressing**. Use a $^1/_4$" seam allowance throughout.*

1. Sew **side borders** to background; press seam allowances toward borders.
2. Sew **top/bottom borders** to background to make the Quilt Top; press seam allowances toward borders.
3. Overlapping edges as needed and working upward from background, arrange prepared appliqués on quilt top; fuse in place.
4. Matching raw edges, layer backing (right side down) and batting. Center the Quilt Top (right side up) on top of batting; pin-baste layers together.
5. Follow **Appliqué**, page 24, to stitch appliqués to the Quilt Top.

appliqué

*Many sewing machines feature a Blanket Stitch similar to the one used on our projects. Refer to your owner's manual for machine set-up. If your machine does not have this stitch, try some of the decorative stitches your machine has until you are satisfied with the look of your appliqué. **Note:** Because the stitches go through all layers of the quilt, you are appliquéing and quilting at the same time.*

1. Thread sewing machine with general-purpose thread that matches or coordinates with applique; use general-purpose thread that matches muslin in bobbin.

2. Set sewing machine for a medium (approximately $1/8"$) stitch and a short stitch length. Slightly loosening the top tension may yield a smoother stitch.

3. Begin by stitching two or three stitches in place (drop feed dogs or set stitch length at 0) to anchor thread. Most of the Blanket Stitch should be on the appliqué with the right edge of the stitch falling at the outside edge of the appliqué. Stitch over all exposed raw edges of appliqué pieces.

4. (*Note:* Dots on **Figs. 5 – 11** indicate where to leave needle in fabric when pivoting.) For outside corners, stitch just past corner, stopping with needle in background fabric (**Fig. 5**). Raise presser foot. Pivot project, lower presser foot, and take an angled stitch. Raise presser foot. Pivot project, lower presser foot, and stitch adjacent side (**Fig. 6**).

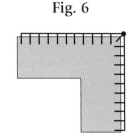

Fig. 5   **Fig. 6**

5. For inside corners, stitch to the corner, stopping with needle in background fabric (**Fig. 7**). Raise presser foot. Pivot project, lower presser foot, and take an angled stitch. Raise presser foot. Pivot project, lower presser foot and stitch adjacent side (**Fig. 8**).

Fig. 7   **Fig. 8**

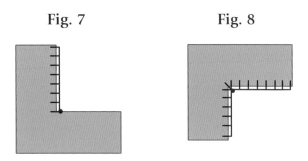

6. When stitching outside curves, stop with needle in background fabric. Raise presser foot and pivot project as needed. Lower presser foot and continue stitching, pivoting as often as necessary to follow curve (**Fig. 9**).

Fig. 9

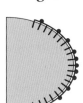

7. When stitching inside curves, stop with needle in background fabric. Raise presser foot and pivot project as needed. Lower presser foot and continue stitching, pivoting as often as necessary to follow curve (**Fig. 10**).

Fig. 10

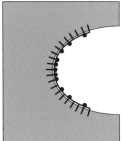

8. When stitching outside points, stop one stitch short of the point. Raise presser foot. Pivot project slightly, lower presser foot and make one angled Stitch 1. Take the next stitch, stop at point and pivot so that Stitch 2 will be perpendicular to the point. Pivot slightly to make Stitch 3. Continue stitching around appliqué (**Fig. 11**).

Fig. 11

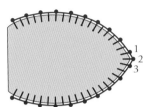

9. End by stitching two or three stitches in place (drop feed dogs or set stitch length at 0) to anchor thread.

adding a hanging sleeve

Attaching a hanging sleeve to the back of your wall hanging before the binding is added allows the wall hanging to be displayed on a wall.

1. Cut a 19" x 5" rectangle of fabric.
2. Press short edges of fabric piece $1/4$" to wrong side; press edges $1/4$" to wrong side again and machine stitch in place.
3. Matching wrong sides, fold piece in half lengthwise to form a tube.
4. Follow project instructions to sew binding to quilt top and to trim backing and batting. Before stitching binding to backing, match raw edges and stitch hanging sleeve to center top edge on back of quilt.
5. Finish binding quilt, treating hanging sleeve as part of backing.
6. Blindstitch bottom of hanging sleeve to backing, taking care not to stitch through to front of quilt.

attaching binding with mitered corners

1. Matching short ends and using a diagonal seam, sew binding strips together (**Fig. 12**)

Fig. 12

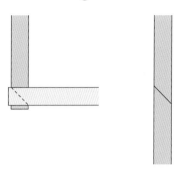

2. Matching wrong sides and raw edges, press strip in half lengthwise to complete binding.
3. Beginning with one end near center on bottom edge of quilt, lay binding around quilt to make sure that seams in binding will not end up at a corner. Adjust placement if necessary. Matching raw edges of binding to raw edge of quilt top, pin binding to right side of quilt along one edge.
4. When you reach first corner, mark $1/4$" from corner of quilt top (**Fig. 13**).

Fig. 13

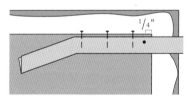

5. Beginning approximately 10" from end of binding and using $1/4$" seam allowance, sew binding to quilt, backstitching at beginning of stitching and at mark (**Fig. 14**). Lift needle out of fabric and clip thread.

Fig. 14

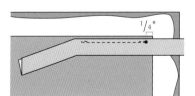

6. Fold binding as shown in **Figs. 15 – 16** and pin binding to adjacent side, matching raw edges. When you've reached the next corner, mark ¹/₄" from edge of quilt top.

Fig. 15   **Fig. 16**

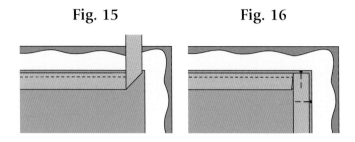

7. Backstitching at edge of quilt top, sew pinned binding to quilt (**Fig. 17**); backstitch at the next mark. Lift needle out of fabric and clip thread.

Fig. 17

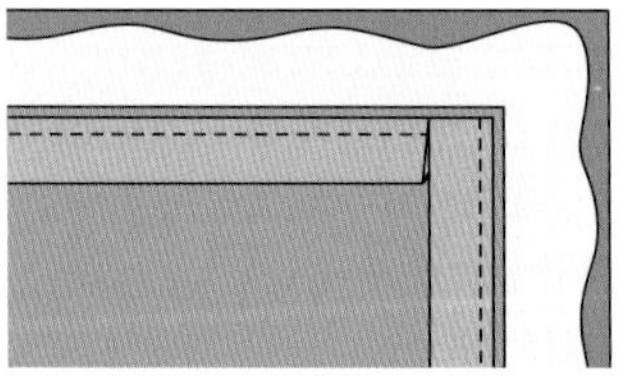

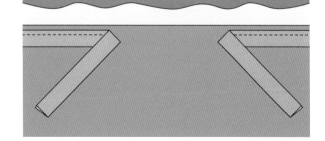

8. Continue sewing binding to quilt, stopping approximately 10" from starting point (**Fig. 18**).

Fig. 18

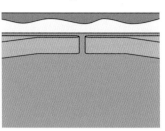

9. Bring beginning and end of binding to center of opening and fold each end back, leaving a ¹/₄" space between folds (**Fig. 19**). Finger press folds.

Fig. 19

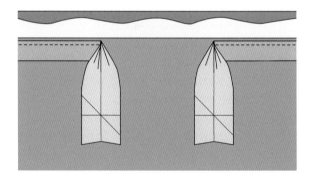

10. Unfold ends of binding and draw a line across wrong side in finger-pressed crease. Draw a line through the lengthwise pressed fold of binding at the same spot to create a cross mark. With edge of ruler at cross mark, line up 45° angle marking on ruler with one long side of binding. Draw a diagonal line from edge to edge. Repeat on remaining end, making sure that the two diagonal lines are angled the same way (**Fig. 20**).

Fig. 20

11. Matching right sides and diagonal lines, pin binding ends together at right angles (**Fig. 21**).

Fig. 21

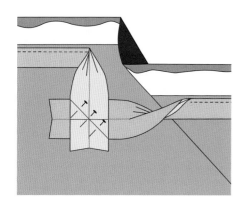

12. Machine stitch along diagonal line (**Fig. 22**), removing pins as you stitch.

Fig. 22

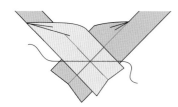

13. Lay binding against quilt to double check that it is correct length.

14. Trim binding ends, leaving a $1/4$" seam allowance; press seam open. Stitch binding to quilt.

15. Trim backing and batting a scant $1/4$" larger than quilt top so that batting and backing will fill the binding when it is folded over to quilt backing.

16. On one edge of quilt, fold binding over to quilt backing and pin pressed edge in place, covering stitching line (**Fig. 23**). On adjacent side, fold binding over, forming a mitered corner (**Fig. 24**). Repeat to pin remainder of binding in place.

Fig. 23   **Fig. 24**

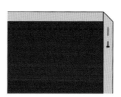   

17. Topstitch in the ditch from front of quilt, catching binding in stitching.

signing and dating your quilt

A completed quilt is a work of art and should be signed and dated. There are many different ways to do this and numerous books on the subject. The label should reflect the style of the quilt, the occasion or person for which it was made, and the quilter's own particular talents. Following are suggestions for recording the history of the quilt or adding a sentiment for future generations.

- Embroider quilter's name, date, and any additional information on quilt top or backing. Matching floss will leave a subtle record. Bright or contrasting floss will make the information stand out.

- Make label from muslin and use permanent marker to write information. Use different colored permanent markers to make label more decorative. Stitch label to back of quilt.

- Use photo-transfer paper to add image to white or cream fabric label. Stitch label to back of quilt.

- Write message on appliquéd design from quilt top. Attach appliqué to back of the quilt.

Metric Conversion Chart

Inches x 2.54 = centimeters (cm)	Yards x .9144 = meters (m)
Inches x 25.4 = millimeters (mm)	Yards x 91.44 = centimeters (cm)
Inches x .0254 = meters (m)	Centimeters x .3937 = inches (")
	Meters x 1.0936 = yards (yd)

Standard Equivalents

1/8"	3.2 mm	0.32 cm	1/8 yard	11.43 cm	0.11 m
1/4"	6.35 mm	0.635 cm	1/4 yard	22.86 cm	0.23 m
3/8"	9.5 mm	0.95 cm	3/8 yard	34.29 cm	0.34 m
1/2"	12.7 mm	1.27 cm	1/2 yard	45.72 cm	0.46 m
5/8"	15.9 mm	1.59 cm	5/8 yard	57.15 cm	0.57 m
3/4"	19.1 mm	1.91 cm	3/4 yard	68.58 cm	0.69 m
7/8"	22.2 mm	2.22 cm	7/8 yard	80 cm	0.8 m
1"	25.4 mm	2.54 cm	1 yard	91.44 cm	0.91 m

Production Team: Technical Editor – Lisa Lancaster; Associate Editor – Frances Huddleston; Editorial Writer – Susan McManus Johnson; Senior Graphic Artist – Lora Puls; Graphic Artists – Amy Temple and Jacob Casleton; Photographer – Ken West.

We have made every effort to ensure that these instructions are accurate and complete. We cannot, however, be responsible for human error, typographical mistakes, or variations in individual work.